Techniques for Marbleizing Paper

Gabriele Grünebaum

DOVER PUBLICATIONS, INC.
New York

Published in Canada by General Publishing Company, Ltd.,
30 Lesmill Road, Don Mills, Toronto, Ontario.
Published in the United Kingdom by Constable and Company, Ltd.,
3 The Lanchesters, 162–164 Fulham Palace Road, London W6 9ER.

Techniques for Marbleizing Paper is a new work,
first published by Dover Publications, Inc., in 1992.
The translation from the German manuscript is by Stanley Appelbaum
with the aid and approval of the author.

International Standard Book Number: 0-486-27156-0

Manufactured in the United States of America
Dover Publications, Inc., 31 East 2nd Street, Mineola, N.Y. 11501

Contents

The numbered items are the 12 specific marbleized papers for which recipes are given.

1. "A Decorative-Paper Maker," copperplate engraving printed by Martin Engelbrecht, Paris, ca. 1740.

4

Introduction

Marbleizing is a craft that is enjoying increased popularity. Known for over a thousand years, it has experienced peak periods in various cultures and regions at different times. The days when marbleizing was a guarded mystery, and its recipes and procedures were transmitted from one generation to the next only under the seal of secrecy, are gone forever.

The basic principle of marbleizing—that the colors are not applied directly to the paper, but are arranged in a pattern as they float on a liquid in a tray and only then are transferred to a sheet of paper laid over them—still exerts a fascination.

In our day people have more and more leisure time and spend more and more of it on craft activities. Modern-day marbleizers, their numbers growing all the time, produce classic as well as innovative and fantasy marbleized papers. The results make it clear that this mysterious, magical craft has lost none of its charm in the course of the centuries.

The ever more frequent museum exhibitions of decorative papers, the ever greater number of publications on the subject and the group activities of marbleizers all show us what is taking place today in the world of "floating colors."

Marbleizing need not be done on paper alone. Fabric, plastic, wood, metal, stone and many other materials and objects, such as sneakers or brooches, have been decorated by means of this mysterious craft.

The present book describing additional methods is a supplement to my earlier Dover book *How to Marbleize Paper* (0-486-24651-5). In this new volume you will find some traditional recipes, but also completely new developments in the field.

With all marbleizing recipes, some of the main ingredients are being patient, keeping calm and taking your time. Please consider the recipes explained here as suggestions that can stimulate your own creativity and joy in experimentation.

The "Decorative-Paper Maker" in the copperplate engraving (Illus. 1) shows us how many papers already existed 250 years ago. Along with marbleized papers many other kinds of decorative papers are depicted: paste papers, printed papers, gold-tooled papers and many more. The lady in the decorative-paper dress is holding a marbleizing comb and seems to be just coming from a marbleizing session.

Now, I don't want to keep from your own session any longer. I wish you a lot of fun as you experiment!

PART I: General Preparations

Workplace, Tools and Materials

Workplace

A clean workplace is needed for marbleizing. A tabletop or a kitchen table will do as a working surface. The surface should be near a water source; a large washtub or bathtub would be desirable. Cover the workplace with paper or foil, or work on a large pane of glass.

Materials

In order to produce classic marbleized papers, you need:
- A large pot for boiling the carrageen moss.
- A small pot for boiling alum.
- A marbleizing tray for the size; it can be of plastic, wood or metal. Beginners would do well to start with a small tray and use larger ones as their skills develop. The tray should be about 2 inches deep and should be of a light color inside so that, while marbleizing, the floating colors can be better recognized and distinguished. It is a good idea to create a separate compartment at one end of the tray with a diagonal partition, so that you can drain off the color residue from the size.
- A metal sieve for straining the carrageen-moss mixture.
- A large linen or cotton cloth, or a nylon stocking, for filtering the size as thoroughly as possible.
- A bucket into which to pour the size.
- A washing or rinsing board on which to lay and rinse the marbleized sheet of paper after it is lifted from the tray. The board must be about 1½ inches larger than the paper on all sides.
- Several small containers for the colors.
- Pipettes (small glass tubes, like eyedroppers).
- Distilled water.
- Strips of newspaper for cleaning the surface of the size. The strips should be an inch or two longer than the width of the tray, and about 2 inches wide.
- Garbage pail.

- Wooden skewers or other thin sticks.
- Several brushes of varying sizes.
- Long-bristled brush.
- Marbleizing combs (see the next section).
- Colors (see that chapter).
- Paper (see that chapter).
- Two pieces of cardboard, somewhat larger than the marbleized papers, between which the mordanted papers will be dried.
- Alum.
- Ox gall (or other dispersing agent; see that chapter).
- Carrageen moss (or other size ingredient; see that chapter).

Marbleizing Combs

The floating colors are arranged in patterns by means of marbleizing combs. There are various types, with widely or narrowly spaced teeth. For some recipes several combs of differing fineness are needed.

But it is also possible to use a single marbleizing comb with variable, or changeable, teeth. With such a comb you can change the number and spacing of the teeth yourself to suit the pattern you want.

Marbleizing combs can be obtained in art-supply stores or by mail order, but you can also easily make them yourself.

INSTRUCTIONS FOR MAKING MARBLEIZING COMBS (ILLUS. 2 & 3)

You will need:
- A wooden board 2 inches wide by 1 inch deep, and 2 inches longer than the width of the marbleizing tray.
- Hairpins with a thick head, or nails of a similar size, for the teeth.
- A drill.
- Wood glue.
- Varnish.

Simple Comb. To make a simple comb, drill a row of holes an equal distance apart. The width of the holes should allow the teeth to fit in tightly. For the fine comb the teeth should be about ⅛ to 3/16 inch apart; for the coarser comb, about ¼ inch. The teeth should be parallel to one another and should protrude on the bottom, by about 1¼ inches. To prevent wobbling, they can be fastened securely with a drop of glue on each.

Comb with Variable Teeth. For the comb with variable teeth, the teeth are merely inserted and not firmly anchored or glued. Drill the holes as directed for the fine comb and, if you need a greater distance between teeth, use only every other or every third hole. Then you can add or remove teeth to suit the situations and patterns.

Double Comb. To make peacock marbleized papers, it is advisable to use a comb with two parallel rows of teeth, staggered so that each tooth faces a space in the opposite row (see Illus. 3). The distance between teeth in a row, as well as the distance between the rows, should be about 1 inch.

In every type of comb, the length of a row of teeth is about 1 inch less than the width of the tray. The projecting toothless edge makes the comb easier to hold.

To make the comb last longer and to waterproof it, the wood should be given at least two coats of varnish.

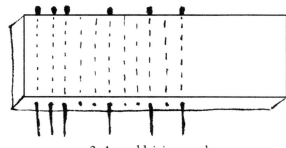

2. A marbleizing comb.

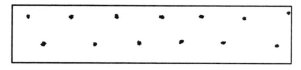

3. Top view of a double comb for peacock marbleized paper.

Paper

Marbleizing calls for a paper with a rough surface (it should not be glazed), for instance papier Ingres or a fairly thick Japan paper.

For your first marbleizing experiments use sheets no larger than about 8 by 12 inches. After gaining some experience and skill, you can also work with sheets about 20 by 27 inches, depending on the size of your tray. Real experts are even able to use papers from rolls. But in all cases the sheet should be at least ¾ inch or so smaller than the tray on all sides.

Preparation of the Paper
(Illus. 4)

When the individual recipes call for it, you must mordant the sheets of paper to be marbleized so that the color will adhere properly. This is done by coating them with an alum solution.

To do this, take about 3 ounces of powdered alum or alum crystals and dissolve in boiling water. After the solution has cooled to room temperature, apply it to the sheets of paper with a sponge or broad brush, taking care that no uncoated and damp areas remain. Now lay the sheets flat one on top of the other between two large pieces of cardboard for drying, weighing them down with heavy books or weights so that they are smooth when work continues.

The mordanting of the paper can also be done a few days in advance, or a steady supply can be prepared.

4. Alum crystals and brush for applying the solution.

Marbleizing Size

Plain-Water Size

Simple marbleized papers can be made using a plain-water size. For this all you need is a tray full of water.

Before you begin, it is important to let the tray stand long enough for the water to be at room temperature, completely calm and motionless.

Paste-and-Water Size

To achieve better control of the color pattern on the size, it is useful to make the water a little thicker and more sluggish. This can be done with paste. You will need:
- 4 heaping tablespoons of (cellulose) wallpaper paste.
- 5 quarts of water.

Dissolve the paste in 1 quart of water and stir energetically. Then thin the solution evenly with the remaining water.

These proportions should be taken as typical only. The thickness of the paste-and-water size (that is, the amount of paste you put in) depends on the colors you will use and the patterns you wish to create.

Carrageen-Moss Size (Illus. 5)

The classic marbleizing size is made from a brew of carrageen moss, also called Irish moss (*Chondrus crispus*). Carrageen moss is a lichen, one of the common sea algae, that grows on cliffs along the Atlantic, the North Sea and the coast of Ireland.

The brew made with this lichen is especially well suited to the creation of delicate and complex color patterns. Colors patterned on carrageen-moss size usually make the finished paper particularly bright and clear.

The dried moss that I use is brownish and like rather soft horn, and gives better results than the gray or off-white moss because of its greater mucilage content. Nowadays it is increasingly possible to find the moss dried and powdered, and it is easier to use this way. Purchased carrageen-moss powder must be handled as directed on the particular package; it is not necessary to boil it, strain it, etc.

MAKING THE SIZE FROM THE DRIED CARRAGEEN MOSS

The first preparations for making the carrageen-moss size should be done a day and a half before beginning the actual marbleizing (see the chapter "Schedule," page 12).

5. Carrageen moss—dried and powdered.

Follow the recipes as closely as you can, because even small deviations and imprecisions in the preparation can affect the entire marbleizing process. The ingredients, sequence, amounts, temperatures and thoroughness in straining and filtering the brew are all significant.

To make about 5 quarts of carrageen-moss size you need:
- 2–3½ ounces of dried carrageen moss.
- 5 quarts of water.

Place the carrageen moss in about 2½ quarts of cold water, put this in a cooking pot on the stove and bring it to a boil slowly. After it has boiled for about 3 minutes, add the remaining water and stir the brew well.

Let the mixture cool for a while, then strain it through a fine sieve into a bucket. Wrap the sticky residue left in the sieve in a cloth and wring out the cloth carefully to squeeze out every bit of the residue. Make sure that no solid parts of the plant get into the bucket. In case this does happen, filter the liquid again.

The filtered size should now be left to cool for about 12 hours and should then be poured into the tray through a fine linen or cotton cloth. In the tray the size should be about 1 inch deep.

Let the carrageen-moss size sit in the tray at least 12 more hours. For marbleizing it should be at about room temperature.

A Few Things to Remember: (1) The thicker the size is, the more easily you will be able to create patterns with the colors floating on it and the more dispersing agent must be mixed with the color for it to spread on the surface. (2) The more colors are already floating on the size, the more dispersing agent must be mixed with every additional color.

Colors and Dispersing Agents

To create marbleized papers you can use different types of color depending on the recipes. To lower the surface tension of the colors, so that they float on the liquid surface and do not intermingle, all colors are combined with a dispersing agent. Which agent, and how much of it, to add to the individual colors depends on the recipe in question, and must be tested in each case.

When you are ready to prepare the colors, it is a good idea to have handy for a test a small tray or bowl with a portion of the marbleizing size—whether plain-water, paste-and-water or carrageen-moss size. Otherwise, a lot of preliminary color testing will quickly use up the marbleizing size, or the bottom of the tray will soon be soiled by a lot of sinking colors.

The amount of dispersing agent to be mixed with a color also depends on when—at what point in the color sequence—that color is added to the pattern. For example, if three colors are used, the first color applied might be mixed with 5 drops of ox gall, the second with 10 drops and the third with 15 drops. The later a color is added, the more dispersing agent must be mixed with it.

There are two basically different sets of colors and dispersing agents for marbleizing: marbleizing colors, to be mixed with ox gall, and oil colors, to be mixed with turpentine.

Marbleizing Colors / Ox Gall

COMMERCIAL MARBLEIZING COLORS AND OX GALL

For Turkish-style marbleizing, only water-soluble colors are used. Many crafts and art-supply stores or mail-order firms offer prepared marbleizing colors that either can be used directly or must be diluted with water (see the instructions that come with the colors).

For centuries the dispersing agent used for Turkish marbleized papers has been purified ox gall, which can be purchased in art-supply stores.

Some commercial marbleizing colors already contain some ox gall (see the instructions supplied by the manufacturer); to others ox gall must be added expressly.

HOMEMADE OX GALL

Some experts and professionals spare no time or effort, and prepare this important marbleizing ingredient themselves.

Take:
- 1 quart of fresh ox gall (obtainable at a slaughter-house).
- ½ pint of pure alcohol.

Shake this mixture well and set it aside for two or three weeks. During this time all gelatinous and fatty substances in the gall settle to the bottom, and the gall becomes thin and a transparent brownish yellow or greenish in color. Once the gall is pure and clear, the clear liquid is filtered through a paper filter and can then be used for our purposes.

HOMEMADE MARBLEIZING COLORS

It is also possible to make the marbleizing colors yourself. All water-soluble colors, such as watercolor, gouache or tempera, are suitable provided they contain very finely ground pigments. The pigments are stirred into a fine paste with distilled water and diluted until they fall from the brush in drops. For these colors to float on the marbleizing size, ox gall must be added to them in any case.

PREPARING THE COLORS FOR MARBLEIZING

A little of the liquid marbleizing color is carefully stirred with ox gall, drop by drop, in a small bowl. Then the first floating trial is made. You can try out the individual colors in a testing tray or plate filled with marbleizing size.

With a brush you let a drop of the diluted color fall onto the size. You can tell if you have the right mixture by seeing whether the color spreads on the water surface, and from the way it does so. Without a dispersing agent, or if too little of it has been added, the colors immediately sink to the bottom. If too much ox gall has been added, the color "explodes" outward into a huge circle. When you release a drop of color onto the size, the drop should spread out about 2 inches.

GENERAL GUIDELINES

Unless the recipe specifically states otherwise, the size and the colors should be prepared a day in advance and left in the space where you will do the marbleizing so that they will reach the same temperature. This is an important prerequisite for successful marbleizing.

Oil Colors / Turpentine

Colors with an oil base are available in various forms, as artist's oils, printer's colors, offset colors or other lithographic colors.

Artist's oil paints for painting usually have the finest pigments and are generally best suited for marbleizing. Art-supply stores and firms offer a variety of colors in small tubes. Some printing colors are also appropriate for marbleizing; but every color needs to be tested individually for the purpose.

For a dispersing agent as well as an oil-color thinner you can use turpentine, turps substitute, pine-tree oil, pine resin or petroleum.

An amount of oil color the size of a lentil is poured into a small container and stirred well with thinner. First you add, drop by drop, enough dispersing agent to liquefy the color, continually stirring well. Then you make the first floating test. With a brush you let a drop of the thinned color fall onto the marbleizing size. You must adjust the mixture according to whether the color spreads on the water surface and according to the way it does so.

If the drop of color sinks to the bottom, you have not added enough dispersing agent. If the color does float on the surface, but produces only a small circle, you should carefully add more dispersing agent drop by drop. If the color, when hitting the size, pulls wide apart, it has too much dispersing agent in it. In that case, the marbleizing color must be thickened a little more with additional oil color. It is best if the color spreads into a circle about 2 inches in diameter.

The Marbleizing Process

The procedure used in a workshop that produced Turkish-style papers over 200 years ago, as well as the necessary steps involved (still necessary today), can be seen on a copperplate engraving from the *Encyclopédie* by Diderot and d'Alembert (Illus. 6). From left to right: Fig. 2 is preparing the colors; Fig. 5 is placing a sheet of paper on the tray with the floating colors and thus transferring the pattern; Fig. 3 is using a brush to drop marbleizing colors onto the size; Fig. 4 is combing the floating colors with a marbleizing comb; in the background, Fig. 8 is hanging up the finished marbleized sheets to dry; and Fig. 1, at the far right, is preparing the size.

Applying and Patterning the Colors

Once you have made several tests and have arrived at the proper mixture of colors and dispersing agent, you prepare the other materials for applying the colors to the size.

How you do this is a matter of taste. Some people swear by pipettes; others prefer wooden sticks, normal long-bristled brushes, artist's or Chinese brushes, or even a marbleizing comb (Illus. 7).

Whatever you use, make sure that each color has its

6. "Marbreur de papier" (Paper Marbleizer), from the *Encyclopédie* by Diderot and d'Alembert, 1765.　　11

7. Marbleizing comb and a variety of brushes.

own equipment for stirring and applying, so that the colors do not get mixed together.

There are basic choices of procedure when you start applying the colors. In one method, you start by applying one color as a background for the rest of the pattern. This is done by means of a long-bristled brush or a small stiff brush like a toothbrush whose bristles flick many very small drops of color onto the size. This application of color gives an irregular effect at the outset, but as you proceed the color is forced back, becoming the background of the pattern.

The second possibility is to very accurately drop two or more colors in alternation onto the center of an already floating color circle. In this way you get one or several "striped circles" (concentric circles of different colors).

Another possibility is to begin directly with the application of colors for the final pattern. For the flower pattern this means beginning directly with the colors for the petals, and so on.

When you have applied enough colors to the size, you can manipulate these colors. Depending on the type of marbleizing size, the creation of precise patterns can be done with combs, sticks or chemicals. The individual recipes in Part II will indicate the specific ways and means.

Laying and Lifting the Paper

As soon as you think that the floating pattern is ready and should be captured as is, you transfer it to paper.

This takes some practice. The side of the paper onto which the pattern is to be transferred (the side treated with alum) should be placed downward. Grasp the two opposite corners with your two hands. Then place one short side on the tray and unroll the paper slowly and evenly (see Illus. 6, Fig. 5).

When doing this it is important for the paper to touch the size at all points with no air bubbles between the paper and the size. At any spot where the paper is not resting directly on the colors, the pattern is not transferred and you end up with an ugly white blotch on the paper. It is sufficient if the paper rests on the colors only a few seconds.

To take the paper out, grasp it by the corners of one short side and lift it carefully out of the tray. Now place the sheet on the rinsing board that is in readiness and rinse it carefully with a stream of clear, cold water. In this way the excess size and the unfixed color residue are washed away. Next, you remove the paper and either hang it up to dry on a line or lay it flat.

If you are working with Japan paper or some other very fine and thin paper, you can use a cylindrical stick to help lift it so that the damp paper does not tear. This stick should be about 4 inches longer than the width of the tray and should have a diameter of at least ¼ inch.

After the sensitive paper has been placed on the tray, lay the stick on the paper, carefully flip the two corners of one short side over the stick, and use the stick to lift the sheet slowly out of the tray without touching it yourself.

Cleansing the Size

At the outset of every marbleizing session and after marbleizing each sheet of paper, the surface of the size must be cleaned and drained off. This is done as follows: Have ready a strip of newspaper. Draw it through the tray in such a way that all particles of color still floating on the surface are pushed together to one side. If your tray has a separate overflow arrangement, push the floating residue into it; otherwise, lift out the residue with another strip of newspaper.

Schedule

Morning of the day before the marbleizing session: Boil the carrageen moss.

Two hours later: First straining of the carrageen-moss size (into a bucket).

In the evening: Second straining of the carrageen-moss size (into the tray), preparation of the colors, preparation of the workplace and assembly of the tools and materials, coating of the paper with alum (the coating can be done even farther in advance).

Morning of the session day: Mix the colors with the dispersing agent and make tests.

Now you are ready to go!

Classic Turkish Marbleized Paper _____

General Instructions

Size: Carrageen-moss.
Colors: Marbleizing colors.
Paper: Mordanted paper.

As early as the sixteenth century, marbleized paper was being made in the Near East. For all Turkish-style marbleized papers the same basic ingredients are used: carrageen-moss size, water-soluble colors and ox gall.

First, drop or spray a background color onto the size. Using a long-bristled brush—which you dip into the color, then wipe off the excess—you fling little drops onto the size until the surface is evenly tinted. (In most historic papers a light beige was used as background color.) Only then do you begin to create the patterns for the individual papers.

If you wish to put the individual ornaments directly on the size, without a color background or undercoating, omit the first step (the application of the background). But in doing so, keep in mind that the colors laid on first always spread most and farthest, so that it is more difficult to draw them into patterns.

It is impossible to describe every variant in marbleizing. Look on the following recipes as stimuli for developing your own ideas and using the technique of "floating colors" imaginatively.

The following sections explain step by step how some marbleized papers are made.

8. Flower-pattern marbleized paper.

1. Flower-Pattern Marbleized Paper (Illus. 8 & 9)

Size, Colors and Paper: See "Classic Turkish Marbleized Paper."

Other Materials: Long-bristled brush; brushes; a few thin wooden sticks.

Recipe: In eighteenth-century Turkey flower-pattern marbleized papers were already in use as decorations bound in between texts in books. Traditional flower-pattern papers generally have a monochrome background. This is created by first spraying the background color onto the size with a brush (see page 12).

Begin the formation of the flowers with the blossom, working from the outside inward. First lay down the petals. Let one drop each of various colors fall one after the other onto the same spot, producing a "striped circle." Using a stick, manipulate this circle artistically into the desired form. Do this very carefully and slowly so as not to disrupt the size. When the petals are the right shape, lay down the center of the blossom by stippling a drop of color onto the center. This drop will spread out into a circle. In case this disturbs the petals already laid down, it is generally still possible to correct them at this stage by means of the sticks.

When the blossom is done, use a thin brush or stick to add the stem and the leaves. These colors should not contain much dispersing agent—just enough to keep them from sinking to the bottom. Dip the brush very slightly into the size and draw the color into the correct form directly with the brush as if you were painting. For the leaves, drip small quantities of color on either side of the stem. For the further detailed work, such as the elaboration of the stem and leaves, use the sticks again.

As soon as the flower or flowers are the way you want them, put away the colors and transfer the pattern to a sheet of paper (see that chapter and section).

9. Flower-pattern marbleized paper, Wiener Werkstätte, ca. 1920.

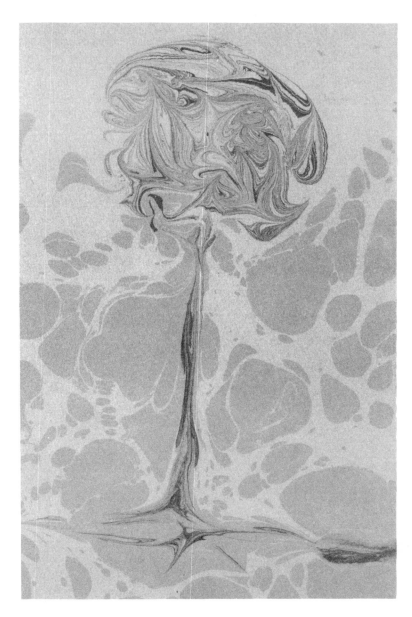

10. Turkish marbleized paper: tree.

2. Turkish Marbleized Paper: Tree Patterns (Illus. 10)

Size, Colors and Paper: See "Classic Turkish Marbleized Paper."

Other Materials: Long-bristled brush; brushes; a few thin wooden sticks.

Recipe: Marbleized trees, landscapes and animals are imaginative modern developments of the classic Turkish flower patterns.

Trees are patterned similarly to the floral ornaments. If desired, the background color is applied first (see p. 12) and only then do you proceed with the actual object.

First the treetop: With one or several different tones of green you apply tiny dots of color which should spread very little. You can also use a small stick to give further patterning to a few of the dots, or to combine or interlace them.

Next you "paint" the tree trunk by applying the appropriate color with a brush and drawing the shape. The colors with which you "paint" in this way should contain just enough ox gall to keep them from sinking. If too much dispersing agent is added, the color will expand in a circle and will displace the color patterns already achieved.

Especially beautiful patterns and three-dimensional effects result when you use different shadings of a single color and apply them in freely conceived patternings.

15

3. Turkish Marbleized Paper: Animal Patterns (Illus. 11 & 12)

Size, Colors and Paper: See "Classic Turkish Marbleized Paper."

Other Materials: Long-bristled brush; brushes; a few thin wooden sticks.

Recipe: Marbleized animals were especially popular with the decorative-paper artists of the Wiener Werkstätte in the 1920s. These artists achieved perfection in this field and created real masterpieces (Illus. 12).

For such a painstaking, delicate task the marbleizing size should not be too thin. The thicker the size, the better you can "paint" and manipulate colors on the surface without having the colors splatter in all directions.

Particularly when it comes to designing marbleized animals it is advisable to paint in a single-color background (see page 12). This not only has the advantage of consolidating the form; in addition, when a background color is already floating on the size, the other colors can be more easily patterned and manipulated.

There are no limits set to your imagination when you create marbleized animals. The two examples shown here are merely suggestions. You can do frogs, fish, snails, other birds and much more—it all depends on you.

11. Turkish marbleized paper: owl.

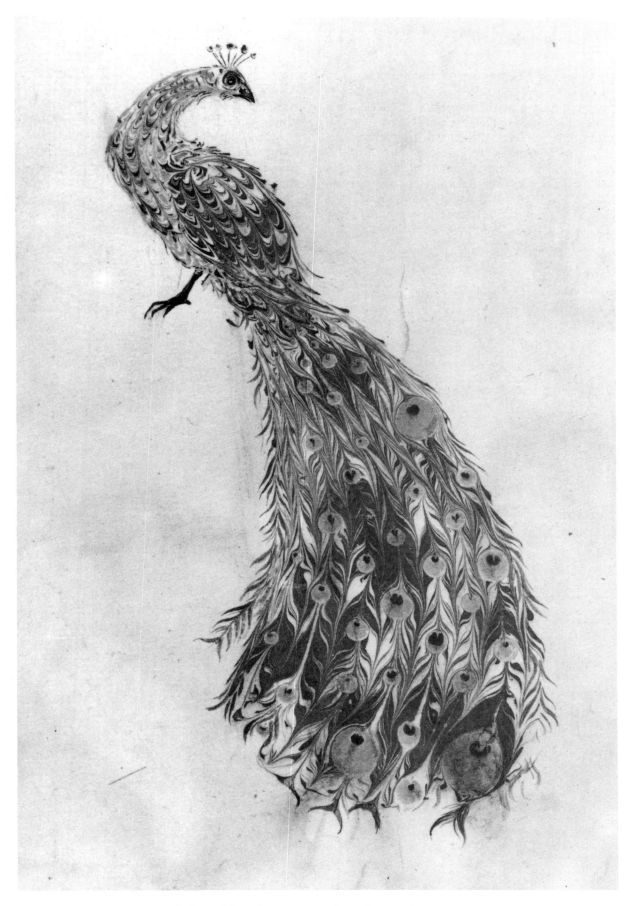

12. Turkish marbleized paper: peacock, Walter Ziegler, ca. 1920.

4. Turkish Marbleized Paper: Landscape Patterns (Illus. 13)

Size, Colors and Paper: See "Classic Turkish Marbleized Paper."

Other Materials: Long-bristled brush; brushes; a few thin wooden sticks; marbleizing comb.

Recipe: It is not very difficult to marbleize landscapes. The motto here is, "less is more." Use the colors sparingly and place only a few details in the picture.

You will achieve an even color background for your landscape if you begin by dripping a background color, mixed with a lot of dispersing agent, onto the size in large drops until you have covered the entire surface (see page 12). The same procedure can also be done with two colors—one for the sky, dripped only onto the upper half of the tray, and one for the ground, on the lower half of the tray. Only then do you add other colors.

Use various shades of a single color to achieve three-dimensional effects. Also keep in mind that the color at the inside of a drop of color is darker and becomes lighter toward the outer rim. You can use these properties and peculiarities of color to imaginative advantage and as possibilities for your creativity.

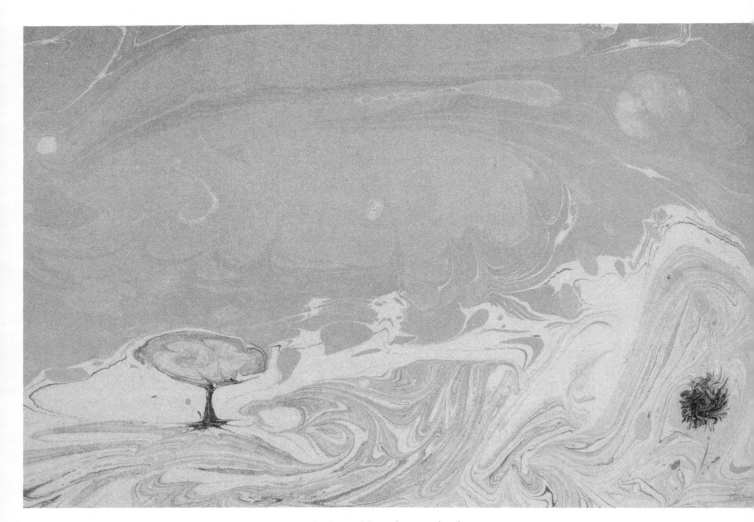

13. Turkish marbleized paper: landscape pattern.

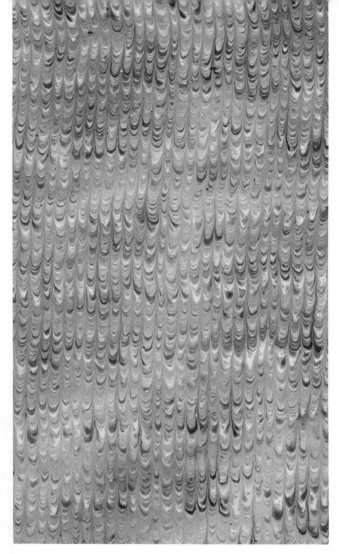

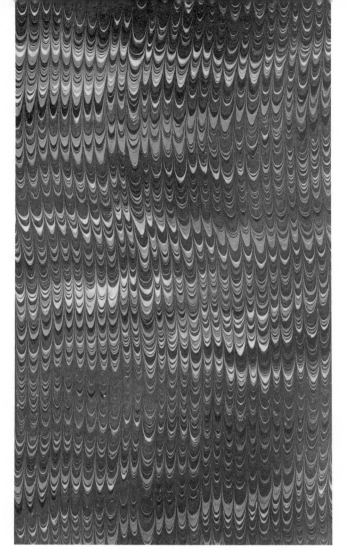

14. Nonpareil (simple combed) marbleized paper.

15. Nonpareil marbleized paper.

5. Nonpareil (or, Simple Combed) Marbleized Paper (Illus. 14–16)

Size, Colors and Paper: See "Classic Turkish Marbleized Paper."

Other Materials: Long-bristled brush; marbleizing comb.

Recipe: Traditional combed marbleized papers, in accordance with old recipes, are usually made with four or five colors. The colors are applied unevenly in alternation until the surface of the size is saturated with colors (see page 12).

Then the floating colors are pulled across the surface from left to right with a comb. In doing this, the comb is placed parallel to one side of the tray and about ¼ inch from the edge. It is dipped slightly into the size and colors and carefully drawn through the tray to the other side. Be careful to use even and slow movements so that no waves arise on the size and the colors do not get mixed up.

Illus. 14 shows a simple combed pattern that was produced in two steps after the colors were laid down (diagram in Illus. 16):

1. Arrows from right to left.
2. Arrows from top to bottom.

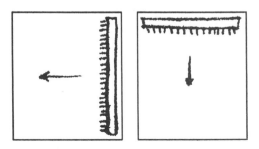

16. Nonpareil marbleized paper: procedure in two steps.

6. Wavy Combed (or, Wave) Marbleized Paper (Illus. 17–19)

Size, Colors and Paper: See "Classic Turkish Marbleized Paper."

Other Materials: Long-bristled brush; two marbleizing combs with different tooth spacing, or one marbleizing comb with changeable teeth.

Recipe: The basic pattern for creating wavy combed patterns is the traditional simple combed pattern (see the preceding section).

The wave pattern is achieved by an additional step. Take a comb with widely spaced teeth and, with gentle wavy motions, draw it lengthwise (from top to bottom) through the prepared pattern.

In this way you get a very lively wave pattern that can be varied depending on the magnitude of the waves.

Diagram in Illus. 19:
1. Arrows from left to right.
2. Arrows from top to bottom.
3. Arrows from top to bottom, with wavy motion, using a coarse comb.

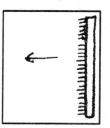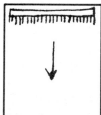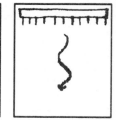

19. Wavy combed marbleized paper: procedure in three steps.

17. Wavy combed (wave) marbleized paper.

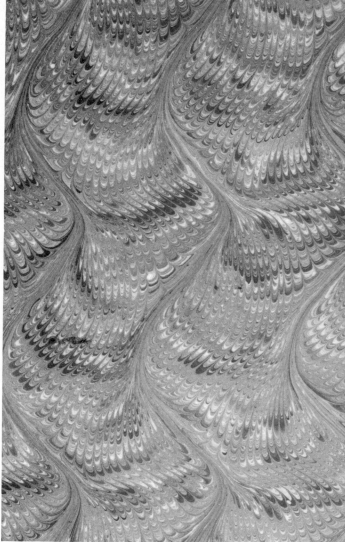

18. Wavy combed marbleized paper.

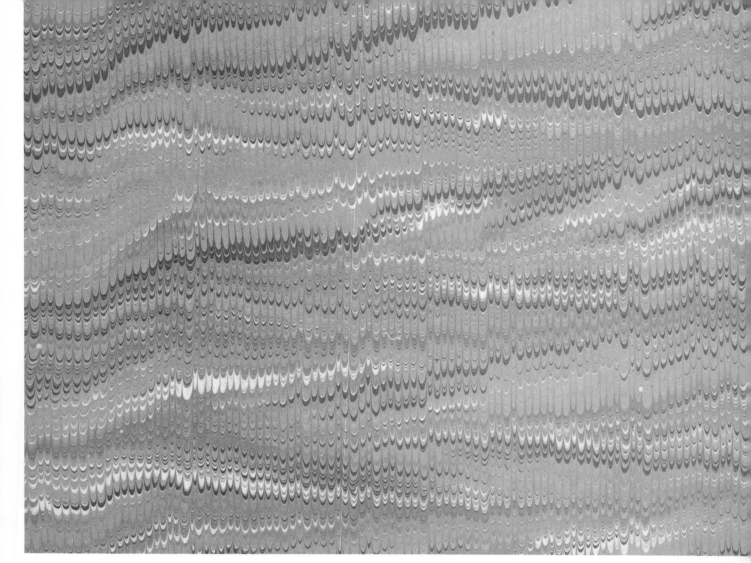

20. Old Dutch (zigzag; double comb) marbleized paper.

7. Old Dutch (or, Zigzag; Double Comb) Marbleized Paper
(Illus. 20 & 21)

Size, Colors and Paper: See "Classic Turkish Marbleized Paper."

Other Materials: Long-bristled brush; two marbleizing combs with different tooth spacing, or one marbleizing comb with changeable teeth.

Recipe: To create a zigzag comb pattern, begin the laying on of colors according to the classic recipe for simple combed marbleized paper (see section 5).

For the first steps in the procedure use a marbleizing comb with teeth at least ¾" inch apart. First draw the colors from left to right, then lead the comb back from right to left—shifted upward or downward by one half tooth-interval.

Finally take a fine marbleizing comb and draw it through the colors in a straight line from top to bottom.

Diagram in Illus. 21:
1. Arrows from left to right.
2. Arrows from right to left—with a shift.
3. Arrows from top to bottom.

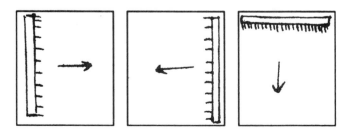

21. Old Dutch marbleized paper: procedure in three steps.

21

8. Spanish Moiré Marbleized Paper (Illus. 22–24)

Size, Colors and Paper: See "Classic Turkish Marbleized Paper."

Recipe: Spanish moiré paper has a pattern of irregular waves ("broken shadows") rather than straight diagonal ones.

The typical patterns of Spanish moiré papers are created when the floating pattern is picked up by a sheet of paper that has been folded into diamonds or squares before it is placed on the tray. The irregular waves are produced when the folds in the paper push together and thicken the colors here and there.

When placing the paper on the colors you need a very steady hand and a lot of experience. The danger in laying down the previously folded paper is that the paper cannot be rolled out with sufficient evenness and air bubbles form between the paper and the size. Wherever bubbles form below the paper, white blotches form in the pattern.

Take a sheet of paper and fold it several times as indicated in Illus. 24. Then smooth it out by hand the best you can. Rub the paper flat on the table, pull it gently over the edge of the table or press it down with a weight for a few hours. The folds should not stick up or project, but should be clearly recognizable and tangible in the paper.

You should practice doing "dry runs" of laying down of such prepared paper a few times before you transfer a color pattern onto a sheet. What is important is a steady hand and the very even rolling out of the paper onto the size.

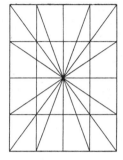

24. How to fold a sheet of paper for creating a Spanish moiré pattern.

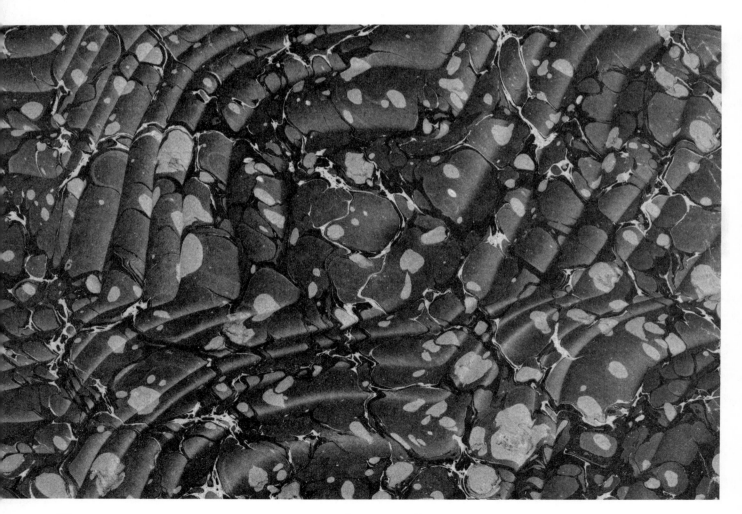

22. Spanish moiré marbleized paper.

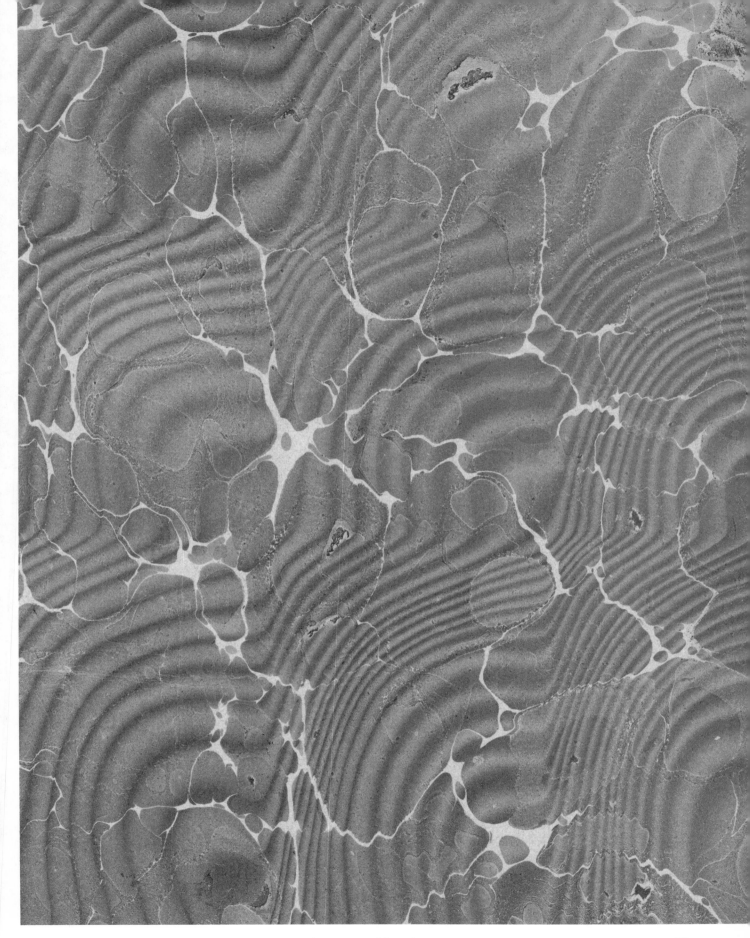

23. Spanish moiré marbleized paper.

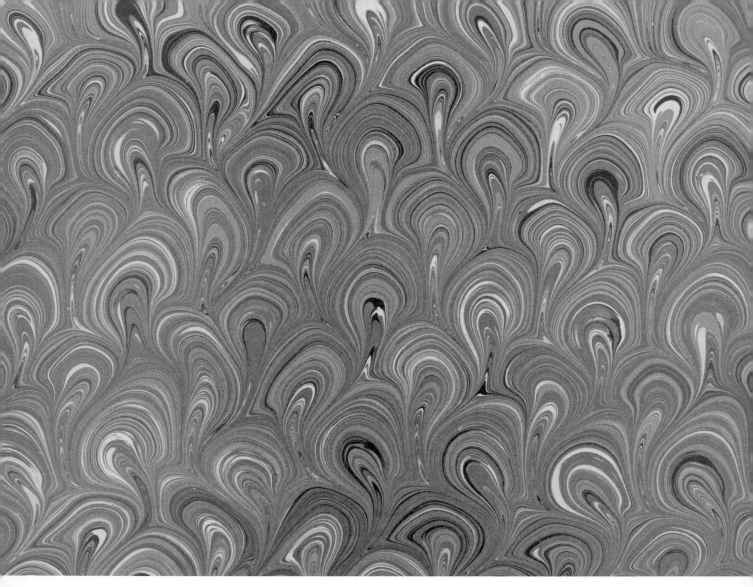

25. Simple peacock (eye) marbleized paper.

9. Simple Peacock (or, Eye) Marbleized Paper (Illus. 25 & 26)

Size, Colors and Paper: See "Classic Turkish Marbleized Paper."

Other Materials: Long-bristled brush; a fine marbleizing comb and a double comb.

Recipe: The basic pattern for creating a simple peacock paper is the traditional nonpareil pattern (see section 5).

To create a simple peacock pattern, start out by manipulating the floating colors just as if you were going to make a combed (nonpareil) pattern. Observe that in every case the final comb movements, done with a fine comb, go across the tray from side to side.

Then you draw the double comb lengthwise through the tray in zigzag wavy lines.

Depending on how broadly or finely patterned you

want your peacock paper to be, you use larger or smaller wavy motions. Diagram in Illus. 26:

1. Arrows from top to bottom.
2. Arrows from left to right.
3. Arrows from right to left.
4. Arrows from top to bottom in a zigzag (with a double comb).

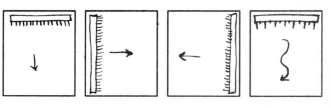

26. Peacock marbleized paper: procedure in four steps.

Suminagashi Marbleized Paper

General Instructions

As early as the seventh century A.D. suminagashi ("ink floating") papers were produced in Japan. They are considered to be the forerunners of Turkish marbleized papers. The unmistakable character of these enchanting patterns arises through a combination of the actual chemistry of suminagashi papers (the typical ingredients) and the mental attitude of the marbleizer.

Size: Water. For suminagashi, plain water is used for the size (in contrast to the coagulated size used for Turkish papers or the paste-and-water size used for certain oil-color papers). Some professional marbleizers believe that spring water gives better results—try it yourself.

Colors: Ink used for calligraphy (in cakes); inkstone. In the creation of suminagashi papers ink is used that is well absorbed by the paper.

Use a cake of ink and rub it with a little water on the inkstone until you have prepared enough very fine liquid ink (Illus. 27).

Often the liquid ink mixed with water will already float on the size. If not, add dispersing agent drop by drop.

Dispersing Agent: Can be turpentine, pine resin, pine-tree oil or ox gall.

Paper: The papers used for suminagashi should be highly absorbent. They should not be treated in advance. Usually Japan papers are used, but they are very thin and hard to handle (see also page 12).

Other Materials: Long-bristled brush; fan; inkstone.

Recipe: To make suminagashi paper the primary requisite is great inner and outer calm. Traditional suminagashi makers look upon their work as meditation and relief from tension. Every emotion, they say, is registered in the pattern on the paper.

Despite the requisite calm and peace of mind, alertness and deftness are needed in the procedure. If the inks float too long on the water, they break up into small particles and the pattern becomes gritty.

Just as in classic Turkish marbleizing, a sheet of paper is laid onto the water surface and the color is transferred directly to the paper.

After the sheets are lifted out of the tray, they are spread out flat or hung up for drying. They do not need to be rinsed and should not be handled any further.

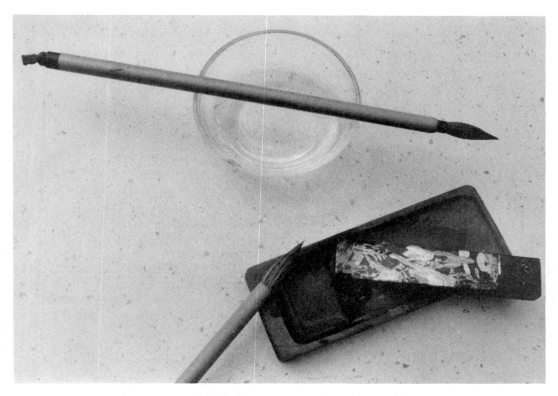

27. Ink, dispersing agent, brushes.

28. One-color suminagashi paper.

10. One-Color Suminagashi (Illus. 28)

Recipe: The water in the tray is mirror-smooth, absolutely calm and motionless. Be careful not to bump into the tray or table unintentionally.

You have prepared the ingredients and achieved inner calm, and can now proceed with the marbleizing:

In front of the tray are one small container with the prepared and tested color and another small container with pure, undiluted ox gall. You need two brushes, one for the color and one for the ox gall.

Take a brush in either hand and dip them into the containers in front of you, the right-hand brush into the right-hand container and the left-hand brush into the left-hand container. Wipe the brushes so they do not drip.

Choose the center point of your pattern, make the first color dot at that point, and then, in alternation and maintaining a constant rhythm, dip the two brushes into the center of the first color circle. The tips of the brushes should penetrate the water surface very slightly. The longer you hold the brushes in the water, the more color will be distributed. You thus create a "striped circle," an alternation of color circles and intervals. Take care that the brushes do not touch one another.

Now you can manipulate the applied color by moving the water. You can do this by blowing on it, stirring it with a fan or causing gentle waves on the water surface in some other way. As you do this the color rings will curl and change.

When your pattern is completed, lift it off with a sheet of paper (see page 25).

11. Multicolor Suminagashi (Illus. 29)

Recipe 1: To make multicolor suminagashi paper, you prepare two or more different inks. With at least two colors it is possible either to create a multicolor design or to use one of the colors as a background.

The materials, two containers with different colors and the tray of water, are ready in front of you. The container with the ox gall or other dispersing agent, together with the corresponding brush, should be set aside.

As in the one-color recipe, you once again work with both hands and two brushes. Instead of ox gall and color you now use two different colors in alternation. Every time you touch the water with the brush, a circle forms on the water surface. As you dip both colors in alternation—each time into the center of the already existing circle—you get a two-color "striped circle" (concentric rings). This is especially charming when the colors are distributed differently over the water surface.

After you have applied enough color, the color circles can be manipulated by setting the water surface in motion very carefully.

Recipe 2: Another classic suminagashi method calls for the use of the two colors completely independently of one another in a single pattern.

Begin by applying the first color to the size, making it the background of the pattern. Then, as in Recipe 1, the second color is applied in alternation with ox gall. This develops concentric circles, which push the originally applied color into the background.

Now you can move the circles into irregular patterns by blowing or fanning (see also Recipe 1).

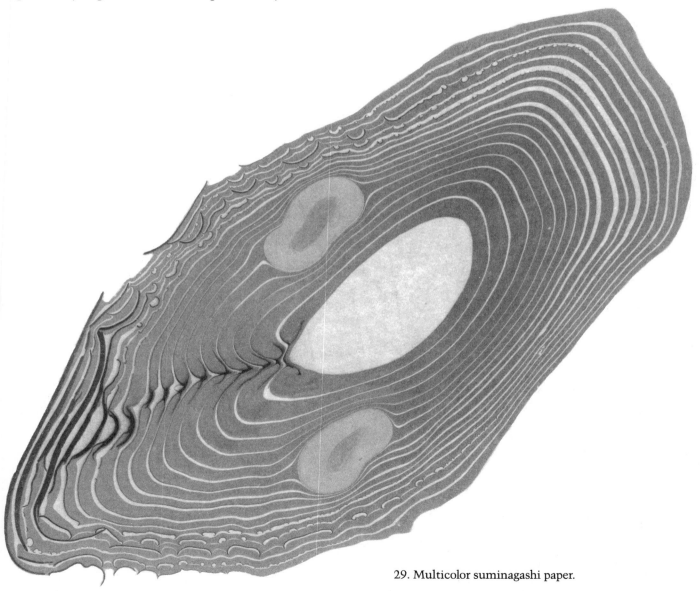

29. Multicolor suminagashi paper.

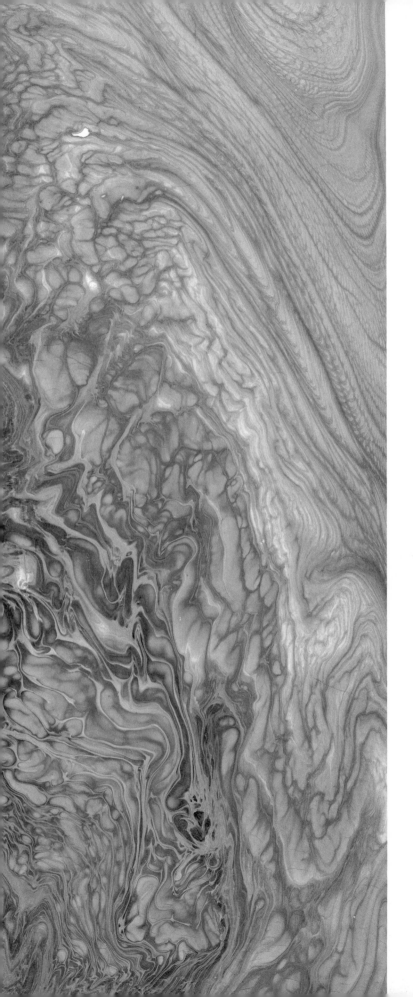

Modern Marbleized Paper

The development of marbleized paper is unbroken. After the invention of "floating colors" over a thousand years ago, the recipes in remote Japan and later those in the Near East were regarded as being shrouded in mystery. They were inherited family secrets and not accessible to the public.

This changed only within our century. A marbleizing magazine regularly publishes new developments and modern recipes and stimulates marbleizers' pleasure and joy in experimentation. With time marbleizers have developed their own specialities, experimenting freely with new ingredients and materials: even a small deviation from a classic recipe can produce completely new patterns.

A contemporary example is here given to show how new ideas influence paper patterns. You should look on this not merely as a model to follow but also as a stimulus for testing your own ideas and developing new types of marbleized paper.

12. Crash Marbleized Paper
(Illus. 30–33)

Size: Plain-water, or thin paste-and-water.
Colors: Oil colors.
Paper: Firm, close-textured paper (should not be treated in advance!).
Other Materials: Oil of turpentine or some turpentine substitute as dispersing agent; you may also want a mask to cover your nose and mouth.
Recipe for Beginners: The secret of crash marbleized papers is that the colors gain an active life of their own when placed on the size. This is due to the significant difference in temperature of the ingredients.

You must work swiftly to make crash papers. During the whole process the colors are in constant motion on the size (even without input from you) and the patterns keep changing.

The size, whether plain-water or paste-and-water, should be several degrees warmer than the colors.

This can cause unpleasant vapors when the dispersing agent is strongly mixed with the steam from the water. Therefore you should work outdoors or in a very well ventilated room, or should wear a mask or use some other ventilation system.

The simple version, which requires no technical equipment, calls for the use of warm water as size. Pour

30. Crash marbleized paper.

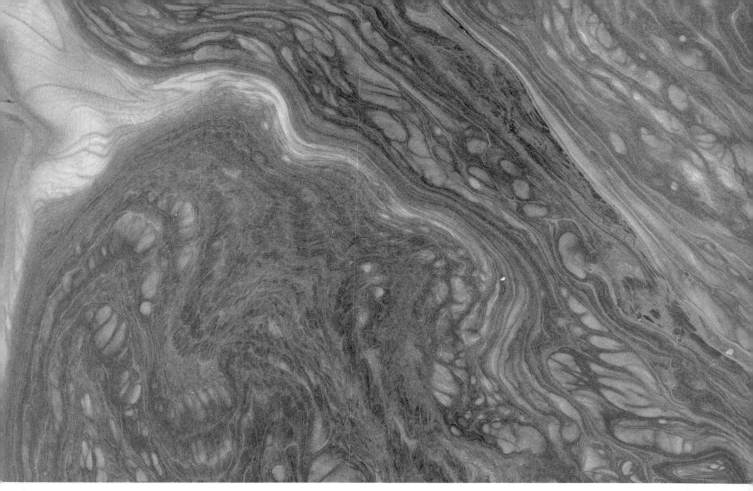

▲ 31. Crash marbleized paper.　　　　　　　　　　　　　　▼ 32. Crash marbleized paper.

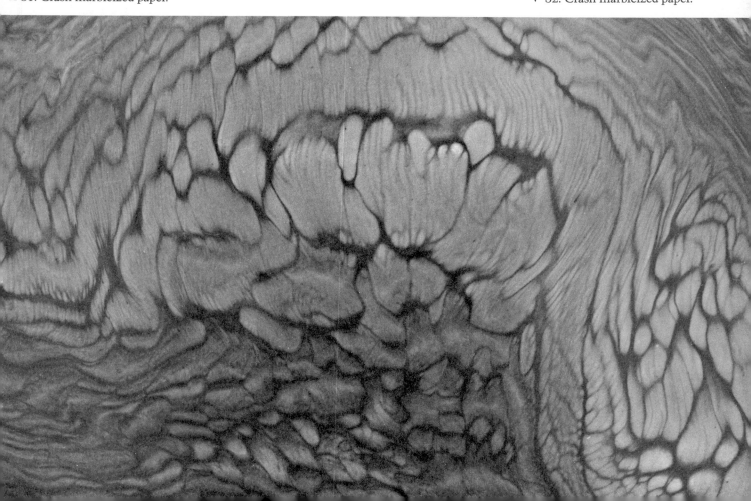

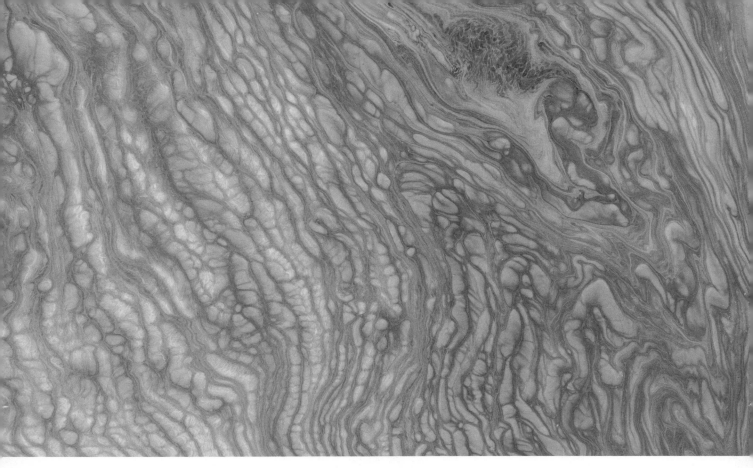

33. Crash marbleized paper.

warm water into your tray and, as in "normal" marbleizing with oil colors, drip the diluted colors, mixed with dispersing agent, onto the size one after the other. Because of the difference in temperature, the colors take on a life and movement of their own. They expand violently and quickly and can scarcely be manipulated.

In some cases the colors also react with one another, producing very interesting patterns.

The laying down of the paper must be done briskly. Since the colors are in constant motion, there is the danger of air bubbles forming rapidly under the paper and causing white blotches.

Advanced Crash Marbleized Paper

Size, Colors and Paper: See "Crash Marbleized Paper."

Other Materials: Marbleizers who wish to expand their knowledge of this technique will need a zinc marbleizing tray, a hot plate and a thermometer.

If you want to produce similar patterns or a series of matching sheets, you must be able to control the temperature of the size and keep it constant.

This is best achieved by using a zinc tray that you place on a hot plate. At the edge of the tray a thermometer (of the bath type) shows the temperature. Place the tray on the hot plate a few hours in advance so that the size is heated through evenly. Before you begin, stir the water well and wait until the waves have settled. Now you can apply the colors.

The colors are applied in the same way as for easy crash papers (see the preceding section).

Usually, the warmer the water, the less dispersing agent needs to be mixed with the colors. But in specific cases this depends on the quality of the colors, the temperature of the water and the type of dispersing agent. Your own experiments and taste should decide which colors in which amount of dilution react most beautifully.

A small clue: in making the papers illustrated, we heated the water to about 100° F and mixed artist's oils from the tube with oil of turpentine in the ratio 1:1.

PART III: Practical Advice

Mistakes and Their Causes

Problem: The colors draw together again after they begin to spread out.
Causes: (1) The size was not well skimmed; a film has formed, or dust has settled, on the surface.
(2) The size is too fresh or is beginning to jell.
Solutions: (1) The surface of the ground must be carefully cleaned off with a strip of paper.
(2) The size must be vigorously stirred.

Problem: Despite the dispersing agent, the color fails to spread or sinks to the bottom of the tray.
Causes: (1) The size is too thick.
(2) The size is warmer than the room.
Solutions: (1) Dilute the size with water.
(2) Let the temperature of the size reach room temperature.

Problem: A film forms quickly on the size, which makes the color placed on it take on jagged forms, partially sink and run off the paper.
Cause: The room is too warm and the size is colder than the room.
Solution: The temperature of the size must match room temperature; neither should be too warm.

Problem: The color gets gritty.
Cause: The size is too thick.
Solutions: (1) Try various dilutions of the size in a small cup and test the colors again.
(2) Dilute the colors with water.

Problem: White blotches appear on the paper.
Cause: Air bubbles between the paper and the size.
Solutions: (1) Roll out the paper carefully onto the size so no air is trapped between the paper and the colors.
(2) The paper has not been evenly treated with alum: either too much alum has been applied to some spots, or some parts of the paper were missed during the application.

Problem: The color does not adhere to the paper, but washes off when the paper is rinsed.
Causes: (1) You failed to treat the paper with alum.
(2) You laid the wrong side (not the alum side) of the paper onto the size.
(3) The paper was too wet when you laid it down.
Solutions: Be sure to apply alum evenly to the paper and to lay the alum-coated side onto the colors. The paper can be slightly damp or dry but not wet.

Problem: The colors flake off when the paper dries.
Causes: (1) The alum solution was too strong.
(2) The paper was dried too quickly and with too much heat (e.g., on a radiator).
Solutions: Use the proper concentration of alum and let the paper dry slowly.

List of Supplies

Marbleizing materials can be obtained in many art-supply stores, where you will usually find not only the colors and ox gall, but also a selection of further supplies: trays, combs, paper, sponges, etc.

There are dealers who specialize in marbleizing supplies. They can provide a large selection of different colors and ingredients, some of them specially prepared for fantastic results. In case no such specialist is located in your vicinity, you can order supplies by mail. Here are addresses of experienced and reliable mail-order suppliers:

Talas
213 West 35th Street
New York, NY 10001-1996

Decorative Papers
P.O. Box 749
Easthampton, MA 01027

Ink & Gall is the only periodical in the world devoted to marbleizing. Published since 1987, it issues two journals and two newsletters per year. The journals feature two marbleizers who write about themselves and provide samples of their work, which are tipped in. Here you will find a lot of information and addresses. Polly Fox, the founding editor, offers workshops every spring and summer and privately by appointment. The address of *Ink & Gall* is: Box 1469, Taos, NM 87571 (phone 505-586-1607).